# MY PHILOSOPHY FOR SUCCESSFUL LIVING

Jim Rohn

**No Dream Too Big Publishing**
*Melrose, Florida*

**FREE Download of a premiere Jim Rohn audio from Download-Jim-Rohn.com**

Published by:

No Dream Too Big Publishing
No Dream Too Big LLC
PO Box 1220
Melrose, FL 32666 USA

www.Download-Jim-Rohn.com

ISBN-13: 978-0-9838415-9-3

# Table of Contents

# Foreword

*by Vic Johnson*

My great friend, Bill Rosselle, introduced me to Jim Rohn in the 1990s through a tape set that he loaned me. Needless to say, my life hasn't been the same since.

Like so many others experienced, it was Jim's simple wisdom that always spoke to me so strongly. And having had the privilege to spend some time with Jim personally, it was the kind of wisdom he lived. Unlike so many of the so-called heroes of today, this hero — an icon of the grandest sort — walked his talk.

I once calculated the time he would have to spend to travel, prepare and speak to the more than 6,000 audiences and 4 million hungry souls worldwide that he reached; and I concluded that he literally gave his adult life to help others find that "day that turns your life around."

I was almost 50 years old by the time I met Jim, but he's one of those kind of people that you feel like you've known your whole life. There was nothing apparently pretentious about him. He felt no need to impress.

I have Kyle Wilson, who was the Founder and President of Jim Rohn International, to thank for the relationship. Kyle also made it possible for me to speak at Jim's event as well as Jim speaking at several of ours. It was some of the highest points of my life when we spoke together at our Claim Your Power Now event in Dallas and he appeared again at our Claim Your Power Now event in Atlanta.

But I will always cherish above those, the interview I got to do with him for our Goals2Go TV show. We recorded it on the first day (I think it was the second show I did that day) and I was fighting a major cold, nervous and excited all at the same time. But he was Jim. Acting like the guy who had spoken to 6,000 audiences, it was just another day at the shop to him. And that, along with his quiet encouragement, put me at ease.

Even today I listen to Jim's audios and it's like he's standing there sharing that "Idaho farmboy wisdom" with me. I've met very few people in my life who could put life in the simple perspectives that Jim could.

They don't make 'em like Jim anymore. And I hope you'll enjoy this book that we put together from Jim's comments at our Dallas event.

**P.S. You can get more of Jim's wisdom with a FREE Download of a premiere Jim Rohn audio from Download-Jim-Rohn.com.**

# Emerging From Your Cocoon

FOR NEARLY 50 WONDERFUL YEARS, I have been in the business of sharing ideas. In that time, several facts have become glaringly obvious. For example, we all want a great deal. This factor holds true no matter what we buy. However, often the most important purchases that we make are not with our dollars, but with our time. This is a fact that many forget, but I always keep this concept firmly fixed in my mind when making presentations.

I have had thousands of people attend my presentations in locations all over the world, ranging from Malaysia and Singapore to Mexico, Russia and Korea. Yet, I have never lost sight of what I see as my two key responsibilities. First and foremost, I want people to always feel as though they absolutely received value for the money that they spent. I want every participant to walk out of one of my presentations saying, "I certainly got my money's worth!"

My second goal in my presentations as well as in this book is that everyone feels that they not only got their money's worth, but also used their time wisely. I want every reader to feel as though the time they spent with this book was time very well spent.

The bottom line is that time is more precious than money. You can always get more money, but you can't get more time. When you spend a day doing something, you have one less day to spend in another way. You can't exactly "earn" that day back later. This means that you always need to spend your time wisely and get the best value for your time that you can.

When you take the time to learn, as you are doing now with this book, you are investing in you and your future. The reason for this is that one good idea can effectively change your entire life. Stop and think about that for a moment. One good idea can transform your whole future, ranging from your health to your finances to your relationships.

Ideas are funny in that they tend to have resonating effects. In this way, it is almost impossible to calculate what an idea is worth. This is why when you buy a book you are not buying the ideas. The publisher simply can't charge for the ideas. They can only charge for the book. Determining what to charge for the ideas would be impossible. After all, you might make a million dollars from a book that only cost you $9.95, that's just how ideas work. And that's what makes ideas so grand.

Another remarkable fact about ideas and concepts is that you never know when or where you are going to find that resonating idea that radiates out and changes everything for you and your life. The early Christians, for example, were instructed that they should never miss the assembly because that's where they may get inspiration, nourishment and ideas. Important moments can come from the harmonious and unexpected alignment of the right speaker, the right book, and the right idea meeting at the very moment that you are in the right frame of mind to hear it.

The bottom line is that you will never know when that moment will arrive and change your life in the process. Viewed from another perspective, the knowledge and inspiration you need to transform your life may not come all at once, but instead in pieces as part of a process. I have seen this in my seminars where people have received different answers to their questions at different seminars.

Both the written word and the spoken word are what we use to convey those priceless ideas that can change our lives. This is why we should all engage in the sharing of ideas. Ideas are knowledge. When we share knowledge in the written or verbal form, amazing things can happen. When one person conveys knowledge to another person, two things happen. The first is a transformation of the person who listens to a presentation or reads a book or article, but another transformation takes place as well, namely in the speaker or author.

Over the years, it became increasingly obvious to me that when I inspired others, I too became inspired. In this way, there was a remarkable and empowering feedback loop of inspiration that is infectious, inspirational and never ending.

All human beings have the ability to transform like a caterpillar emerging from its cocoon and taking to the sky. This is the essence of personal development: taking information in, becoming inspired by it and allowing yourself to be transformed and, in turn, inspire others as well. Seeing what you can become and what you can help others become is the major challenge in life.

# Chapter 1

# The American Economic Ladder and Girl Scout Cookies

I LEARNED AN INTERESTING economics axiom when I was 25 years old. Essentially, this axiom stated that we get paid for bringing value to the marketplace. The general idea is that no matter who you are, if you bring value to the marketplace, you will be rewarded. This is how the marketplace works. I began my self-education when I was 25, and by the time I was 31 or so, I was a millionaire. I feel that it was due, in part, to the fact that I had embraced this concept wholeheartedly.

Keep the truth about the marketplace in mind. The marketplace isn't some mysterious, unknowable place full of confusion. Instead, the marketplace is comprised of people. But this was just the beginning of my discovery. I learned a two-part, life changing fact. Number one, you will be paid for what you bring to the marketplace, and number two you get paid for what you become.

If you become a leader, a supervisor or an entrepreneur, you will get paid for that contribution. As I mentioned above, you get paid for what you bring and you get paid for what you become. It is important to remember that companies, with the exception of monopolies, will usually continue to improve their products. In a similar fashion, you need to remember that you are your own product. Realizing this fact and embracing it is the essence of personal development.

Once I understood the possibilities of personal development, I literally found it difficult to sleep. In fact, for the first year I hardly slept at all. For at that point, I understood a powerful fact: formal education gets you a job, but self-education is what makes you rich!

The importance of self-education and investing in your own personal development is something that you won't learn about in high school or even college. However, I can't stress enough that this is a critical aspect of success.

Let me give you a bit more background about my personal story. I quit school when I was 19 believing that I was smart enough to land a job. Soon after I started a family, however, the money just wasn't there.

The realization that I had to make a change came when I was 25. One day I heard the best sales pitch ever and I wanted to buy the product that was being sold. In this case, believe it or not, the great sales pitch was from a Girl Scout and the product was a $2 box of cookies. The problem was I didn't have the $2 to spare. I told her that we already had all the Girl Scout cookies we could eat. I felt horrible lying to a Girl Scout about buying a $2 box of cookies! At that moment I knew something had to change.

Determined to make that change, I began the process of finding a mentor who would help me transform my life. It was not just a process of finding a way to become wealthy, but a process about developing a philosophy of living and learning how to bring a unique and valuable service to the marketplace.

I found my mentor who promptly began deciphering and debunking all my flawed thinking. He pointed out that my approach from ages 19-25 had simply not worked. He also told me that I desperately needed to abandon my excuses, such as "taxes are too high", and encouraged me to forego my list of excuses. His advice was to list out all of my excuses and then rip that list to shreds. Then get a new piece of paper and put one word on it - "me."

The answer to my problem was to deal with what was within me. He explained to me that the answer to solving my problems wasn't to be found by listing out the obstacles both real and perceived in the outside world, but instead by noticing the obstacles in my own thinking and approach.

This shift in perspective sparked my journey. One of the lessons I learned was that each individual's personal income is determined primarily by his or her philosophy. If you refine and change your philosophy, then everything around you will change as well. This, of course, includes your income. This strategy works and it's amazing!

There is a good reason for the fact that just about everyone wants to come to America and that reason is our amazing Economic Ladder. The American Economic Ladder ranges from people earning a few thousand dollars a year to hundreds of millions! But how can you go from making a few thousand dollars a year to making a few million. That is, well, the Million Dollar Question isn't it? The answer, once again is philosophy.

You could wait for the government to raise the minimum wage, thus adopting what could be considered a philosophy of governmental intervention. However, you will never become a top-earner if you are depending on that to happen. Nor can you depend upon the company you are working for to do it either.

You can try a philosophy of demand where you demand more money from your employer. This might increase your earnings. But will you really become a millionaire in the process? No. Even if you band together with other workers and go on strike, you will never become a top-earner using the philosophy of collective confrontation either. None of these philosophies or approaches will help you achieve your end goal. They just don't work.

It is quite possible in America to become wealthy, but only if you have the correct philosophy. What does work then? What works is the fourth philosophy, which I like to call the philosophy of performance and productivity. With this philosophy, you do what is necessary to improve yourself and your capabilities. You learn to do more and be more.

If you use the Philosophy of Performance and Productivity, the whole economic scale belongs to you, as you have opened up new possibilities for yourself. If you are working for a company you will be more valuable and you will earn more, move up the ladder, have more money and that, in turn, will open up additional opportunities for you. This is potentially a never-ending cycle of benefit. You can go as far as you want to go because the possibilities are endless, especially in America.

If you think doing this is hard in America, think again. The average worker in Bangladesh earns about $200 per year! If you are walking around with the distorted idea that succeeding in America is too hard, then you have the wrong philosophy. That means you need to undergo a process of self-education.

Another misconception is that you can't dramatically increase what you are earning. This also is just wrong. In America, there are people earning $5 per hour. However, you don't have to look very hard to find people earning $50 per hour. Keep looking, and you will soon find those earning $500 per hour, such as a high-powered attorney. You see, it is all about bringing the right goods to the marketplace. And this Prosperity Ladder doesn't end there, but, in fact, just keeps going up. Part of your self-education is to realize that there are possibilities and that they are all around you!

So remember, your income is determined by your ability to wish, envision and re-imagine yourself and your possibilities. The Economic Ladder of America doesn't restrict anyone. In America, you can own as much real estate as you want, as many cars as you want, and as many boats as you want.

Here is the core of the philosophy. It all boils down to this: if you work hard on your job, you make a living. If you work hard on yourself, you can make a fortune. What is the reason for this truth? Success is not something you pursue. Success is something that you attract by becoming an attractive person. The way that you become rich is not by wishing your life were easier, but instead by focusing on making yourself better.

# Chapter 2

# The Philosophy of Performance and Productivity

MANY PEOPLE WANT TO ACHIEVE wealth and greatness. This is a topic that has certainly received more than its fair share of attention over the centuries, and it will continue to do so long after the publication of this work. However, the answer to how to achieve wealth and greatness is surprisingly simple. But many people may not like the message.

Achieving wealth and greatness can be distilled down to helping others. Find a way to serve many people. Simply stated, this is what leads to great wealth, great power and great influence.

One of John F. Kennedy's more famous statements was, "Don't ask what your country can do for you, but what you can do for your country." This quote encapsulates what one needs to do to achieve greatness and financial independence.

Thinking about what you can do for the people in your family, your neighborhood, your state, your country and the world is the secret of wealth. Take Zig Ziglar, for example. I have known Zig for nearly fifty years, and he is fond of saying, "If you help enough people get what they want, you can have everything you want."

Now you might be thinking that this is just too simple to be accurate, but it is. This is the great philosophy that is at the heart of transforming your life. Invest in yourself, invest in your own self-education and then take that knowledge and use it to help others get what they want and need out of life. In the process, you will acquire power and financial freedom.

The world is currently at an extraordinary level of change. All one has to do is look at the metamorphosis that is occurring in China. China now has 235,000 millionaires. And guess where the new billionaires are coming from? India. These are nothing short of extraordinary times, and unparalleled opportunities exist in every country around the world.

A facet of this opportunity is competition. Competition is now becoming truly global for the first time. Within this new element of competition comes a new element of opportunity. Many fear what competition brings, as many will always fear the unknown. But the fact is that without this extraordinary level of competition, all of these new opportunities would not exist.

How can you make sure that you are invaluable in this new, dynamic and ever-changing 21st-century global marketplace? First, make certain that you have more than one skill. Look at the U.S. auto industry over the last 15 to 20 years. Car manufacturers shut down plants and laid off workers at nearly regular intervals. Those without numerous skills lacked the flexibility to compete. In short, the phenomenon of a specialist who works in the same field and in the same way from the age of 21 to 65 is now a rarity.

A variety of skills mean that you are more flexible and can adapt to the whims of a changing and evolving marketplace. After all, that which does not evolve does not prosper and does not survive. By having numerous skills, you are greatly increasing your value and worth in an ever-changing marketplace. Further, with such a dynamic workplace destined to become the norm, you should strive to keep your current skills sharp and periodically develop new ones. This will give you an important edge and one that will help safeguard against obsolescence.

All of this information intimately ties into why I became rich around the age of 31. Soon after I found myself unable to buy that box of Girl Scout cookies, I began investing in myself. That meant learning additional skills.

I wrote down the skills that I had at my disposal at the time, and they were fairly limited. I reflected on my upbringing on a farm in Idaho. I certainly could milk a cow but well, let's just say that didn't pay very well. I knew I needed to know more in order to be more and earn more.

Here is one example of how I diversified my skill set. Believe it or not, I began teaching capitalism in Russia. Once communism had disappeared, I realized there was a real vacuum in the former Soviet Union. Soon I found that my skills in teaching capitalism were of value in Russia. In the last 12 years, for example, I have been to Russia five times helping people make the transition from a centrally planned economy to a capitalist one.

One of the key lessons that I taught my students is that poor people and rich people have wildly different philosophies. For example, here's the philosophy that ensures poverty: spend your money and invest what is left. The bottom line is that this strategy will make you poor.

On the flip side, here is the philosophy that will make you rich: invest your money and spend what is left. You can have the same amount of money, but thanks to a difference in philosophy, you can achieve dramatically different results.

Making money begins with having the right philosophy, but there are other steps as well such as finding your customers and selling them something that you believe in. In my case, it was a nutritional product.

Secondly, learn how to find good people. A business needs good people behind it. You can't do everything. I took my inspiration from the Bible on this one. A Biblical lesson that always stood out in my mind was that if you search you can find good people, but you have to be committed to searching. Taking the time and effort to search for good people will yield the reward of finding quality people. This sounds simple enough, but it's a point that many would-be entrepreneurs and employers often overlook.

At this stage you will have three things. The first will be your skills. These skills will enable you to help people improve their lives. Secondly, you will have found your customers and have a quality product to sell them. Finally, if you have taken the time to seek out quality people, you will have a pool of good people to help you with your endeavor. Now you are ready to make money and change lives; your life and the lives of those around you!

Your employees are key. After all, what could be more important than finding the people that you will work with in order to make your dreams come true? Finding good people can be difficult, and it will take time. If they are independent minded people, you may be in for a challenge, as this can be as difficult as herding cats. Just keep in mind that herding sheep is easy, but you don't want to work with sheep. You want independent minded go-getters!

If you can get two or three people focused on the same task, then almost nothing is impossible. You certainly won't hear that idea taught in the educational system, but it's a fact. This underscores the importance and long-term value of having quality people by your side.

You don't have to be General Motors or Microsoft to make a profit. All you have to do is be reasonably bright, focused, willing to work and then learn how to multiply. Don't be afraid to get someone else out there doing it! This may be harder in some places in the world, but it's easy in America. That part is what makes America unique.

Whatever you set your sights on, if you are the one doing it, you can make a living, perhaps even a good living. However, you want *more* than a good living or you probably wouldn't be reading this book. Get somebody else to do the work, and it's the beginning of a fortune, pure and simple.

Then show someone else how to get rich, show someone else how to earn money, how to sell stuff and how to recruit. You will be amazed just how good this can make you feel. Knowing that you have empowered another person to live his or her own dreams is unlike any other feeling. With the Philosophy of Performance and Productivity, there is a never-ending cycle of benefit and rewards, and there is enough for everyone!

# Chapter 3

# Working With Others

AS YOU MAY SUSPECT by now, finding quality people to work with you and for you is a critical aspect of transforming your life and finding prosperity at the same time. There are more steps in this process, and we'll cover one that can dramatically alter the trajectory of your earnings, namely reward and recognition.

Rewarding people for small steps of progress is a key part in your ultimate success. If you are a parent, then you know that you need to reward your children for their successes, why not do it in business? The simple fact is that rewarding people for small, successful steps can make you a fortune.

Here is what I like to call the Wealth Philosophy and it is as follows: be so busy giving others recognition, that you don't really need it for yourself. (Don't worry, you'll be paid back many-fold for your efforts.)

Next take the time to learn the skill of communication. Becoming a skilled communicator is one of the single best investments you can make in yourself. As a skilled communicator, you will be able to communicate your own needs and motivate your employees. Don't underestimate the importance of this one.

Communicating in a business climate can take several different forms and yields differing levels of reward.

### 1. Training

The first level is training, which is simply showing someone how your business works and how a specific job works. Training is easy. In fact, it is so easy that children can often do it.

### 2. Teaching

The second level is teaching. This is somewhat more complicated. Teaching is using communication to give others skills of their own. If you are a successful teacher your pupil will walk away with new abilities and skills of their own.

### 3. Inspire

Then there is the third level of communication and that comes in the form of learning to inspire. In part, this means helping people envision being better than they currently are. This involves getting people to see beyond the confines of where they are now and to imagine where they could be in the future. This is what can change and revolutionize lives.

Interestingly enough, all of this focus on learning how to communicate better with others serves to make you more money. This all ties into the frenetic pace of globalization as well.

Just as you will need more than one skill for the 21st Century workplace, you will likely need more than one language. This comes as a bit of a shock to a nonlinguistic culture, such as the United States. But many people around the world, such as in Europe and Asia, already speak multiple languages. This gives them an edge.

For example, as you read this book, millions of people are currently learning English in China. When I travel to Scandinavian countries, I don't need a translator. This process is already well under way.

Keep this additional fact in mind. I have numerous colleagues who speak three or even four languages and they are making millions in each language as a result. Communication is key in business, and communication is evolving due to technology. Teaching your children multiple languages is one of the greatest gifts you can give them for the future. Learning additional languages isn't impossible. Like so much in life, it is just a matter of mindset and focus.

If you are still not convinced that learning a foreign language is in your best interest and the best interest of your family, consider this. One of the best ways of building a financial wall around your family is to have more than one skill and more than one language. For example, it is far easier for people to emigrate from one country to the next when they have multiple skills to offer and can offer those skills in multiple languages.

Chapter 4

# A Look at the Fundamentals

IN SCHOOL, MOST PEOPLE hear the mantra of "stay in school, study hard, get a job and stay out of trouble," but I was always left wondering, "Is that it?" Of course, the answer is no. There is more to success than following that simple statement and there are more possibilities than that as well.

Remember it is all about your philosophy and your approach. Here is another concept that made me wealthy: profits are better than wages. Now this doesn't mean that you can't have both, as you can. It's just that profits are better than wages. Wages will make you a living, but profits will make you a fortune. The good news is that you don't have to settle for one over the other.

I began by working for profit and fortune on the side. I was working my full time job, but I also was making strides towards making profits as well. I was working full time on my job and part time on my fortune. This is simple, and it's something that anyone can do.

No matter what you are doing in life, it's important that you learn the fundamentals or the foundation of a given job or task. Without this ability, you don't really know what is going on. Making money is not really any different. Let's take a look at the well-proven fundamentals that you need to know in order to make more money.

First of all be suspicious of anyone that says they have a new system for making money or have "new fundamentals." The odds are that they don't have anything of the kind. The reason is that these fundamentals are time-tested and have been in play for quite some time.

The first thing you need to do is have a personal guidance system of things that you will and will not do, people you will associate with and that you will not associate with, and so on. This guidance system will act as a way for you to stay out of danger and keep on the right side of opportunity. While this may sound simple, in real life situations it can be rather complicated, just like the real world.

Opportunities may come your way that are less than a stellar match, and you may need to go the other way even if they seem attractive for some reason or another. Danger and opportunity after all usually walk side by side. Being proactive and constantly evaluating new information means that you will be able to distinguish between danger and opportunity.

If you don't think that this dynamic between danger and opportunity is alive and well, just look at the recent history of humanity. Most of the world during our lifetime has been dominated by what can only be deemed as outright tyranny. On one side is liberty and on the other tyranny. These two forces have been in a contest over the last 50 odd years. Finally, liberty won more than its share. We saw the walls fall in Berlin, we saw communism end its run and we saw forces of liberty begin to emerge with new dynamism across the globe.

Maybe it hasn't always been easy or pretty, but it has been progress and substantial progress at that. Now much of the world has liberty. Yet, just 50 years ago, most of the world was experiencing tyranny. Once liberty wakes up and goes to work, tyranny is no match for it.

Under communism, Stalin murdered millions in an attempt to make communism work. The West looked at these events in horror. No wonder Reagan called the Soviet Union an evil empire. Under the Soviet system, the state controlled all the capital and this made them too powerful, far too powerful. Stalin, and others like him, had a free hand to do as they pleased, and the results were often horrifying.

We can see this struggle between liberty and tyranny, light and darkness, at play in other aspects of life as well. A good example of this is in the realm of health. You need to keep your body strong and healthy if you are going to achieve your dreams and your goals. This aspect of success is often overlooked, but it is critical for happiness and success. After all, how can you tackle your dreams and desires if you lack energy or even worse are ill?

# Chapter 5

# Refining and Strengthening Your Personal Philosophy

LEARNING FROM YOUR OWN personal experience is a key to success. Being able to turn a failure into a positive experience that you learn from can be the difference between success and failure. In short, learning from your own experiences is critical in refining and strengthening your own personal philosophy.

It is also vital that you learn from other people's experiences as well. This point couldn't be more obvious, but people consistently overlook it. You simply can't experience everything. Taking the time to recognize the experiences, the successes and failures of others can help you achieve what you want in life. You can learn a lot from failures and successes of all sorts, both your own and those of others.

When you take the time to learn from the successes and failures of others, you are learning how to avoid the dangers and maximize the opportunities that the world presents. We can use such information for the purpose of self-education, which is what personal development is all about.

Now, in no way am I telling you what to do. While there is a great deal of advice in this book, it is ultimately up to you to define and decide upon your own unique path. I am only outlining what is possible and letting you know that through the process of personal development and self-education, you can make substantial and tangible changes in your own life.

Keep this in mind: you are not a tree. You are not an immobile object, stuck in one place with virtually no mobility. As a thinking, mobile human with intellect and free will, you can interact with your environment on a high-level. You can take your own personal philosophy, born out of self-education and personal development, and make dramatic changes. These changes can impact the world around you and, of course, your own life as well.

At the core of everything is your personal philosophy; how you will approach opportunity and danger and how you will approach right and wrong. How you behave and interact with the world will define your level of success and even the legacy that you leave the world.

A second factor in redefining and strengthening your personal philosophy is your attitude. It is one thing to understand that you are a dynamic being capable of interacting with the world, but your attitude is also a key component in the process of success and happiness.

We are all affected by what we know, and we are all also affected by how we feel. No matter how stoic you may be, your decisions will be impacted in some way by your emotions. How you feel about your past and your future will influence your decisions and the paths that you select for yourself. Realizing this factor will help strengthen your philosophy and your approach.

So much of accomplishing what you want in life necessitates looking back at our experiences so that we know better how to proceed for the future. Projecting yourself out into the future and thinking about where you want to be. This process can begin with some very simple steps such as writing what you want out of your future.

Taking the time to sit down and write out your goals for the present, the near future and the more remote future is a necessary part of transforming your life. My mentor showed me the value of taking these steps and, in fact, I would even go so far as to state that this is one of the single greatest gifts that you can give another person. Teaching others the value of establishing their goals and moving towards them is priceless.

So stop and ask yourself some important questions:

- What do you want for yourself?

- What do you want for your family?

- What do you want for your business?

- How much are you willing to give?
- How much do you want to share?
- What are your goals?
- Are these goals inspiring?
- How do they make you feel?

Remember that asking questions is how we begin to acquire knowledge both about the world around us and ourselves as well.

Andrew Carnegie said that he was going to spend the first half of his life earning money and the second half of his life giving it all away. Now that is inspiring! Carnegie got so excited about his goal that he was able to earn about $400 million dollars in the first half of his life, which in those days was an amazing amount of money. Then, true to his word and true to his goal, he spent the second half of his life giving it all away.

The main lesson here is that reasons and goals can be powerful. Having reasons and goals can serve as powerful motivators that will not just change your life, but also the lives of those around you and perhaps even the world. So be bold about setting your goals.

Take the time to look back at your own experiences, as they are a potentially rich source of information and self-education. Then look forward with inspiration in your heart about what it is that you seek to accomplish with your life, for yourself, your family and for the world at large.

You can have all you want out of life if you endeavor to help others. If you want to be a powerful and influential leader, then you simply must recognize this absolute fact.

What has made America the most powerful unique nation in the last six thousand years of recorded history is due to all of the gifts from all over the world that have been flowing in here. For the last four hundred+ years, all sorts of people have been coming to America, but they have not done so empty handed. Instead, these people brought their own unique gifts with them. This is what has made America unlike any other place in history. The gift of language, the gift of freedom, the American work ethic, the gift of knowledge in all of its forms, and the gift of inspiration, vision and enthusiasm, have all blended together to make America unique and great.

All these gifts were brought here. That's what makes us so unique. No country has ever been such a depository of knowledge and gifts quite like America. The contribution of every individual makes America unique, whether it came from one of the millions of forgotten slaves and indentured servants or from the nobleman granted a land charter from a king or queen of Europe. One person doesn't make an enterprise, nation or economy. It takes all of us to make an economy.

Finally, work is essential to all endeavors. Great accomplishments like building a nation from scratch come from activity. Having a strong core philosophy is one part of the equation, another is having the right attitude and the third part is "rolling up your sleeves" and putting in the work that is necessary to get the job done.

# Chapter 6

# Your Financial House and Measuring Success

MY FATHER TAUGHT ME the importance of living debt free and being financially independent, and I think that lesson has become more important than ever. With the issue of debt and its impact on people and nations being a front-page issue around the world, taking a moment to consider the importance of avoiding debt is time well spent.

Gaining financial independence has many components and many faces. One of those components is to get excited about your work. This is part of why you need to enjoy what you do. You may have heard that if you enjoy what you are doing, you will work harder and have more enthusiasm for the job at hand. There is great truth in this.

As we discussed in the last chapter, hard work derived from your philosophy is an important part of getting what you want out of life. It is necessary to learn to embrace work, as we can't simply wait for a miracle to arrive and change our fortunes. Instead, we must all take the proactive steps that will lead us to our goals.

Many people, however, will work blindly without taking the time to reflect on their progress. Stopping periodically to access and measure one's progress is a critical aspect to success. Setting a goal, as we have covered, is a central and vital place in the process of achieving your goals and financial independence. However, keeping track of your progress is key.

If you have ever tried to lose weight, then you already understand this idea very well. If you don't stop and weight yourself from time to time to track your progress, then you don't really know how well your weight loss strategy is working. Likewise, without measuring your progress, it will be difficult for you to achieve the financial freedom that you seek.

How many years would you like your child to spend in the fourth grade? More than likely, your answer is one year. We instinctively teach our children to measure time in reasonable increments. After all, the bigger the job, the longer it may take to complete even if you are completely focused. You can't ask someone to perform a complex task then pop back in five minutes later and ask, "How is that coming along?" Keep this in mind with your own efforts.

This issue of time underscores how important personal responsibility is in the process of success and personal development. Society doesn't demand the things from you that will make you financially independent, for example. Society does not demand that you take good care of yourself so that you can be healthy. Nor does society demand that you build a financial wall around your family. There is no law that you do any of these things. This all boils down to personal responsibility, self-education and self-development.

You might suspect that there is a moral judgment in all of this, but that is not necessarily the case. Consider for a moment that a bad person can make great decisions, and a wonderful person can make poor decisions. Your character and moral compass does not necessarily mean that you will make excellent decisions or horrible decisions.

Good people can have temporary lapses in judgment, just like anyone else. Decision-making is more complex than black and white or left and right. However, this factor does highlight the importance of developing your personal philosophy and following it closely. Remember being able to distinguish between danger and opportunity is one of the core elements that we are exploring in this book.

# Chapter 7

# Six Steps for Leading an Extraordinary Life

IN THIS FINAL CHAPTER, I want to discuss lifestyle and our personal relationships. Earlier we discussed communication and its tremendous importance in the realm of business success, but it is important to remember that communication plays a role in your personal life as well.

The more powerful a speaker you are, the more careful and measured you need to be with your words. This is part of living a good life. In fact, everything we have covered in this book in one fashion or another points towards being a positive, contributing member of society. Leading a good life and trying to help others, ranging from one's family to one's community to one's country and hopefully, even the world.

If applied to your life, the principles of this book will enable you to live an extraordinary life, a life that you will find enriching and rewarding and one that will help others prosper and grow as well.

But what constitutes a good life? Obviously, you can get a variety of answers to this question. But I think most people will probably agree with the list that I have assembled.

### 1. Be Productive

First on our list of six steps for leading an extraordinary life is being productive. Here is why: you won't be happy unless you are productive. The core of the word "productivity" is that you produce. Your goal should be to produce something of worth and value for the world. Don't sell yourself short, but instead strive to produce all that you can for your family and your fellow man.

You will feel better about yourself and your life when you are producing and being productive. We all want to feel as though our lives have meaning and significance. One way to find such meaning and purpose is to provide for one's family and for others in the world.

### 2. Value Relationships

The second element necessary for living a good life is to have good friends. Collect and cultivate relationships with people who know you, know what you are about and like you. Many people approach life from the perspective of "me, me and me." However, in the end, these people are usually left sad and alone. When your focus is only on yourself, it is nearly impossible to cultivate real and lasting friendships that will stand up to the test of time. Those who do not contribute to society often find that they pay a price in the form of solitude.

Medical research is strongly indicating that relationships can actually increase your lifespan. With this in mind, why not cultivate quality friendships? Just remember to make certain that the friendships that you do cultivate are positive ones and those friends are a positive force in your life.

### 3. Respect your Origins

The third element on our list is to know your culture, heritage, language and history. Diversity is part of what has made America great. Understanding the contributions of our ancestors to this great multi-cultural and multi-ethnic nature is a must!

### 4. Spiritual Health

Don't forget to take time for your spiritual health. No matter what you believe, it is important to spend time focusing on your spirituality and your beliefs. Don't leave those beliefs unexplored and unstudied. This is part of the process of building a strong country, strong families and strong communities.

It is important to keep in mind that commonalities of beliefs, just like commonalities in culture and language, serve to help societies form strong bonds. Without these bonds, it is difficult for societies to keep a tight and cohesive society over time. It is this commonality of experience and shared identity that helps communities and countries thrive and grow.

### 5. Build an Inner Circle

Fifth, cultivate your inner circle and take the time to inspire your inner circle of friends and family, as this is important for so many reasons. Chief among these reasons is that your friends and family will, in turn, inspire you as well. Having an inner circle of friends and family also can serve to give you a buffer against the expected bumps, bruises and unforeseen consequences of life.

No matter how careful you are and no matter how much you work towards spotting the difference between danger and opportunity, you may occasionally fail. When these moments or other unexpected events occur, it certainly is nice to know that you have friends and family to depend upon and rely upon. Otherwise, life can be a cold and lonely place. Many people often discover this truth once it's too late.

### 6. Plant the Seeds

Finally, we come to God. Now I am an amateur on the topic, but there are a couple of ideas I feel compelled to share. Consider this, God says, "If you plant the seed,

I will make the tree." What an amazing arrangement. God doesn't expect you to make a tree, he just expects you to plant the seed. This is exactly how the process of personal development and self-education works. If you plant the seed, God will do the rest. There is a whole world out there, thanks to God, to help you along. However, we do have to participate in order to see miracles occur in our own lives.

### More Jim Rohn

**You can get more of Jim's wisdom with a FREE Download of a premiere Jim Rohn audio from**

**Download-Jim-Rohn.com**

# A CONVERSATION WITH
# JIM and BOB

IN JULY 2006 Jim Rohn and Bob Proctor were at the top of their careers as icons in the personal development industry. Both had spent four decades speaking to audiences around the world. They had each influenced millions of people at live events and many millions more through their books, audios and videos.

Bob Proctor, Vic Johnson and Jim Rohn
after their only appearance on stage together

Despite all of their travels and thousands of events, neither of them had ever met the other. Vic Johnson, who had been mentored by both men, wanted to change that. So he scheduled one of his Claim Your Power Now weekend events and invited Bob and Jim to speak.

Both accepted, and the stage was set for the one and only time they would ever appear together in front of an audience.

To say it was a magical moment is an understatement. The ages-old wisdom of these two sages was awe-inspiring. Below is the transcript of their conversation.

**Vic:**   Bob, if you had to select the single-most important principle for success, what would it be?

**Bob:**   You really have to focus on the other person you're serving and what you're doing for them. I believe most people are thinking of themselves and not the other person.

**Vic:**   Jim?

**Jim:**   I've been asked the following questions: How is it possible to be the greatest? How is it possible to have great wealth, power, income or influence? How do you get self-respect or respect from others?

The answer is, "He that wishes to be the greatest, let him find a way to serve the many."

So the key is "enlightened self-interest," which means in order to have what I want to achieve in the fullness of my life, I must find ways to serve.

**Vic:** Jim, when you're making a decision, how do you know it's a good one? Or is it just an old paradigm talking to you?

**Jim:** Sometimes you know and sometimes you don't. It all depends.

People look back and say, "I spent too much money and time on that project." So that's part of your education on how to make better decisions.

If it's a high drama decision, you might have to get away [to think]. There's an interesting phrase in the Bible that says every once in a while you should enter your closet and shut the door. Not necessarily to shut yourself in, but to shut everything out for a while.

For me, sometimes the best time to make a decision is to get away from the noise, the traffic, and the family. Not that you don't love everybody and all the activity. But sometimes during decision-making you've just got to get away.

One of my best ways to do that was to ride my dirt bike on the jute trails up on top of the mountains in Northern California when I lived up there. It was a great place to shut the door on everything, and have some quiet time to think things over.

**Vic:**  Bob, how do you know its intuition and not the old paradigm?

**Bob:**  I think you have to understand the difference between your intuitive and reasoning factors, because you're dealing with vibration.

You're saying go to your closet, your sanctum sanctorum. Go to the quiet place within, because that's where the message is coming from.

The answer comes with the question. It's being tuned in enough to hear it. It comes in the form of vibration, and your intuitive factor picks up the vibration.

However, there's a difference between the vibration that's set up by your thinking and the intuitive factors giving you your answer.

I think you can be quiet in a crowded subway, but you've got to be able to block out what's going on outside and go inside. And if you do that, you'll know whether or not you're making the right decision. Your intuitive factor never lies — its Spirit talking to you — and the question and the answer are one in the same.

It's like I always say, a rhetorical question without an answer is a statement. It's like having an inside of a room without having an outside. It's the law of opposites.

I think you have to train yourself. I've been doing it for about as long as Jim, and there aren't many people who've been doing it longer than I have. I work at studying the difference between thought vibration and intuition. You'll get to where you can tell the difference as it's an inner-knowing.

**Jim:** Part of it's taking a chance. To go into any enterprise is to know how to get in, then you have to think how to get out.

I met Neil Armstrong — the first man on the moon — and he said, "Going to the moon, all you had to do was solve two problems. The first was how to get there. The second was how to get back. Make sure you don't leave till you've solved both problems."

**Vic:** Jim, during your journey to success, what has been your greatest obstacle? And how did you overcome it?

**Jim:** That's pretty easy: Figuring things out for myself. The very early part of life is how you walk and talk, how you relate and how you get what you want, which is the game of life.

Trying to understand myself, to grow as fast as possible, to comprehend early instead of late was my greatest obstacle. But I found a way at age 25 how to accelerate my education with the right mentor and made my fortune fairly quickly. I've lost, made and lost a few fortunes since then.

I saw a cartoon about a 12-year-old boy with a little angel on one shoulder and a little devil on the other, and both were whispering in his ears. The little devil said, "Go ahead and do it. It'll be okay." And the little angel said, "No, no, no!"

What was that little voice you heard this morning? *You're running a little late. You don't have to do your exercises today.*

Well, that happens every day as we're all tempted. The light turns red, and you have to make a decision whether to run it because you're running late. Or to be on the side of caution and wait.

As Abraham Lincoln said, "We listen to the better angels of our nature so our life will have more order and success."

**Vic:**   Bob, what's your greatest obstacle?

**Bob:**   My first mentor and coach, Ray Stanford — the one that gave you *Think and Grow Rich* — used to say, "Bob, you're the only problem you'll ever have and you're the only solution." It took me about five years to understand that.

I really believe when a person gets to a point where they understand they're the only problem they're ever going to have, I think the rest of the road becomes pretty smooth. Because if they think there's anything else in their road, they're in trouble. You can't win if you're a victim.

**Vic:**   Bob, if you had one part of your life to re-experience, what would it be and why?

**Bob:** I really enjoy it now, so I don't want to go back and do any of it.

I was watching Johnny Carson one night and George Carlin was sitting in. Vincent Price was on as a guest, and he had just shot a pilot. Carlin asked him, "Well, Vincent, what's the show about?"

Price replied, "It's about a train and I'm the conductor. But this train is a different train. You can buy a ticket and go back to any point in your life you would like to start over. When you get to that point, I can stop the train and let you off, and you can start your life over from there. I think everybody would like to go back and start their life over at some point, don't you?"

Now keep in mind there are millions of people watching, especially the executive producers. Carlin's pulling on his beard and said, "No, I don't think so. If I went back and started anything over, I wouldn't be me. And I like me."

I wouldn't want to change things in my past — and there have been some wild ones — or relive it again. It's made me who I am, and prepared me to do what I'm doing. I love where I'm at!

**Vic:** Jim, how about you?

**Jim:** I've got a long list of unique experiences. I was in Rome one time, and before I was introduced someone said, "Jim Rohn loves the music of Andrea Bocelli," the blind opera singer.

So when I walked up to the podium, all 9,000 Italians stood up and sang one of Bocelli's songs for me in true Italian style with tears and everything.

When I got back home I told this story to my grandchildren. I said, "Here's the scene: A choir of 9,000 and an audience of one. That's the Italians. If you tie their hands behind their back, they can't speak. Their language is so incredibly expressive and unbelievable." It was one of the most unusual experiences of my life. Then I told a group in Pisa that I never met a shy Italian.

One of the greatest experiences was in Siberia where the Russians sang for me in Russian. It was just incredible.

**Vic:** Jim, knowing what you know and if you were 40 years old, what kind of business would you be in today?

**Jim:** I just love real estate, and I've made a lot of money in real estate. I'm sure Bob can relate to this: For every one we made, there was one we passed up.

Nine years ago a friend of mine wanted to sell me his tiny condo in Carmel, California. You couldn't have gotten in the shower, it was such a little bitty place. A one-bedroom efficiency apartment up two flights of stairs in downtown Carmel.

He said, "I want $80,000 for it." And I said, "That's insane. Nobody's going to pay $80,000 for this condo." Even though I wanted one I said, "This is too much money," so I passed.

Later he put it up for sale at $650,000. He thanked the good Lord every night when he went to bed that I didn't buy it. And I wondered why I was so stupid I didn't buy it myself.

Don't buy the second car till you've bought the second house. It's not cars that make you rich, it's houses that make you rich. I love real estate!

**Vic:** Bob?

**Bob:** I'd probably go into network marketing as it's a way you can leverage yourself, you can help a lot of people, you can earn a lot of money and have a lot of fun on your own time. I think it's a great concept.

**Vic:** Bob, how long did it take before you felt it all clicked and you had no more doubt?

**Bob:** About nine years. I was working in Chicago with [Earl] Nightingale. I was winning, but I wasn't satisfied just to win — I wanted to know <u>why</u>. I knew I should have been losing and I had no reason to win. So I found that you can win and not know what you're doing.

I heard about Val Vanderwall, a brilliant guy who ultimately became a mentor of mine. I jumped on a plane and flew out to Vancouver. And as soon as he got up to speak I knew he knew what he was talking about.

I talked to him afterward, and told him I'd like to spend some time with him. He was running to catch a plane, so I said, "It doesn't have to be right now — any time. I've got to catch a plane too."

He asked me where I was going and I said, "Chicago." He said, "What are you going there for?" I said, "I live there."

He says, "What are you doing out here?" I said, "I came up to hear you speak." I think he was impressed that I had traveled so far.

He said, "I'm not going to be in Chicago any time in the near future. I'm going to be in Toronto." I said, "I'm from Toronto, so I'll fly over and meet you. It's only an hour."

We were to spend two or three hours at the Skyline Hotel in Toronto, but we spent three days there.

He was the one who explained the little stick man drawing, and it was a graphic illustration of the mind. It seemed like everything fell into place. I had all the information, but it was scattered. It was like some was here and some was there. It all made sense in part, but I couldn't get it to fit with the subconscious mind. I mean, where is it and what is it? And that got me into studying it.

Then I started to study with Dr. Roder, who knows more about the mind than anybody I've ever met, and I've never stopped studying it.

But that little drawing was when it all fell in place. That took me nine years. I was a serious student then and I still am.

Like Jim was saying, reading just two books a week is going to impact every aspect of your life. I do at least that, and have for a long time.

We were talking one night and I said, "I don't know if it's an awareness, or if it's that you're in tune with it. It seems to get just a little better and runs a little smoother — like it's not even measurable. It works a little better, and then you die."

**Jim:** The difference between a professional and an amateur is if they lose a close game, the amateur probably lets it affect him forever. For the professional it only lasts a few minutes and they say, "Tomorrow night we'll run them off the court." But the amateur lets it linger and linger.

I knew I was getting better when my reaction time was better and faster to some of my losses, and I was saying "I shall recover."

**Bob:** It's like Napoleon Hill said, "There's a difference between wishing for a thing and being ready to receive it." Nobody's ready for the thing, so they believe they can acquire it. And then the secret is that they don't submit to failure. The amateur submits to the failure. The successful person believes they just made a mistake.

**Jim:** Probably the biggest challenge is golf. You make a bad shot. Because you can't wait 30 minutes to do your next play, recovery time has got to be almost right away to put it in its place.

It's like losing a child. I don't know what that's like — it's never happened to me. But you have to find a place to put it. It's going to affect you the rest of your life, but it shouldn't destroy your life.

**Vic:** Jim, should a person's business be based on their passion? Or should it be based on a need in the marketplace?

**Jim:** First, I'd go for the need in the marketplace. Someone said, "To be successful, find a great human need." Second, find the answer to that need. And third, take the quality and quantity of service to as many people as you can reach in your lifetime. So that's pretty simple.

There are some things you can do extremely well and not be passionate about. You can get very rich and not necessarily find your passion, what really turns you on.

You find a job, fill a need, do it extremely well, and fortune is waiting for you. But it may not be high-energy passion that does it.

It's just the simple knowledge of how to acquire something, render enough service to get it done, and inspire enough people to be successful. And you can become successful yourself.

Passion is a whole different subject. Bob, how about you? You've got a lot of views on passion.

**Bob:** You should consider what you're passionate about. I think you should spend your life doing it, but that doesn't necessarily mean that's how you're earning money.

Money isn't made from working; money's made from providing service, which doesn't mean you're working at all. I'm providing a service and earning money in Australia, but I'm not in Australia.

So I think you should work at what you love. Something you're passionate about. But it doesn't have to be where you're earning your money. Now, if you can earn your money there, that's a bonus.

**Jim:** That's an unbeatable combination.

**Bob:** It's a beautiful combination if you're fortunate enough to hit that. But if you're not, it really doesn't matter.

I know people who love to paint and I say, "That's what you should do. Find another way to earn money if you have to." So I'm all for spending your days doing what you love.

**Jim:** Ultimately the greatest passion is to be extremely successful so that you can bless not only yourself and your family, but others along the way.

**Bob:** That's why I think we're so fortunate in this business. If you're thinking of getting in the business, get in and then never quit. I asked Jim, "Do you ever plan on quitting?" He said, "No. I'm never going to quit."

**Vic:** Bob, the ship is going down and they're going to the lifeboats. You know you're going to land on a deserted island and it's going to be a while before they pick you up, but you can only carry one book with you. Which book are you carrying and why?

**Bob:** I would take *Think and Grow Rich*. That's the book I carry with me all the time. I carry a number of beautiful books that would probably do the job, but I'm just so connected to that one.

Jack Canfield was going to get me to auction it off once, and I thought, *Oh, God. No!* I say if you won't lend something you should give it away because you don't own it — it owns you. And so I'm obviously owned by the book.

**Vic:** Which one for you, Jim?

**Jim:** Obviously for me, the Bible. It's a collection of 66 books, so it's a nice library and a great study on contrast. And a great study of the lives of some people to admire, and the lives of some people to despise. It's a great source of ideas, intrigue, information, illustration, and inspiration.

It's not just a 20-page book; it's got a lot of content, enough poetry to keep you dazzled, and enough history to keep you intrigued. And enough glimpse into the future to keep you wondering how it's all going to work out.

The Master teacher, who was so good at telling stories, said, "The Kingdom of heaven is like..." He didn't say "The Kingdom of heaven is..." That probably would have been too abstract or too beyond our ability to comprehend.

He said, "It's like a husband and wife. It's like a family. It's like a bride and a bridegroom." Always relating it to life. And what life was like was probably the best illustration of what the Kingdom is like.

Throughout the whole Bible from beginning to end it keeps you intrigued about people's lives and how they solve their problems, and economic, social, personal, religious, spiritual information. So that would be it for me.

**Bob:** It's a good sales manual too!

**For a free print book of Napoleon Hill's classic**
***Think and Grow Rich,***
**go to: Get-My-Free-Book.net**

## Books from Laurenzana Press

*The Strangest Secret* by Earl Nightingale

*Memory Improvement : How to Improve Your Memory in Just 30 Days* by Ron White

*Persistence & Perseverance: Dance Until It Rains* by The Champions Club

*The Law of Attraction: How To Get What You Want* by Robert Collier

*Time Management Tips: 101 Best Ways to Manage Your Time* by Lucas McCain

*Get Motivated: 101 Best Ways to Get Started, Keep Going and Finish Strong* by Lucas McCain

*Successful & Healthy Aging: 101 Best Ways to Feel Younger & Live Longer* by Lisa J. Johnson

*Self Confidence Secrets: How To Be Outgoing and Overcome Shyness* by Lucas McCain

*Happiness Habits: 21 Secrets to Living a Fun and Outrageously Rewarding Life* by Lucas McCain

*Self Help Books: The 101 Best Personal Development Classics* by Vic Johnson

*Overcoming Fear: 101 Best Ways to Overcome Fear and Anxiety and Take Control of Your Life Today!* by Lucas McCain

*Public Speaking Fear? 21 Secrets To Succeed In Front of Any Crowd* by Lucas McCain

*Going Green : 101 Ways To Save A Buck While You Save The Earth* by Lucas McCain

*Stress Management : 101 Best Ways to Relieve Stress and Really Live Life* by Lucas McCain

*Should I Divorce? 11 Questions To Answer Before You Decide to Stay or Go* by Jennifer Jessica

*Divorce Recovery: 101 Best Ways To Cope, Heal And Create A Fabulous Life After a Divorce* by Lisa J. Johnson

*Should I Have a Baby? 10 Questions to Answer BEFORE You Get Pregnant* by Jennifer Jessica

*Stop Procrastinating: 101 Best Ways to Overcome Procrastination NOW!* by Lucas McCain

*Think and Grow Rich : The Lost Secret* by Vic Johnson

*Should I Get Married ? 10 Questions to Answer Before You Say I Do* by Jennifer Jessica

*Meditation Techniques: How To Meditate For Beginners And Beyond* by Lucas McCain

*Fast NLP Training: Persuasion Techniques To Easily Get What You Want* by Lucas McCain

*How To Attract a Woman: The Secret Handbook of What Women Want in a Man* by Jennifer Jessica

*Cure Anxiety Now! 21 Ways To Instantly Relieve Anxiety & Stop Panic Attacks* by Lucas McCain

Made in the USA
Middletown, DE
15 April 2018